The Forward book of poetry
2006

The Forward book of poetry
2006

FORWARD
LONDON

First published in Great Britain by
Forward Ltd · 84–86 Regent Street · London W1B 5DD
in association with
Faber and Faber · 3 Queen Square · London WC1N 3AU

ISBN 0 571 22995 6 (paperback)

Compilation copyright © Forward Ltd 2005
Foreword copyright © Tim Dee 2005

Reprographics by Icon
Printed by CPI Bath
Lower Bristol Road · Bath BA2 3BL · UK

A CIP catalogue reference for this book
is available at the British Library.

To Oliver McTernan

Preface

LIKE MANY, I was greatly saddened to hear last September of the premature death of Michael Donaghy. He was a gifted poet with a musician's ear for rhythm, a generous champion of new poets and ever a charming and courteous man. Michael won the Forward Prize for Best Collection in 2000 with *Conjure*, and then three years ago chaired our judging panel – it was typical that his foreword for the anthology that year should have talked not only of the influence of Auden, but of spontaneity and imaginative daring, of the integrity of the poetic line and of his acquaintanceship with an art forger. He is much missed and, appropriately in such a strong year, we are delighted that the prize for Best Single Poem should be dedicated to his memory.

No two years' submissions for the Forward Prizes are the same, and the shortlists, and the choosing of them, can cause reactions that range from the passionate to the derogatory, the critical to the ebullient, even occasionally (dare I say it?) a stifled yawn. This year it was generally felt that the quality, in particular from newly published poets, was encouragingly high. Certainly the choice fuelled the judges with enthusiasm (even if it did entail long judging sessions), and my thanks go to each of them: Maura Dooley, Michael Symmons Roberts, Romesh Gunesekera, Claire Armitstead and, chairing them admirably, Tim Dee.

My thanks go also to the many people who contribute in different ways to the prizes and this anthology, including Felix Dennis, Jules Mann and her team at The Poetry Society, Gary McKeone and his team at Arts Council England, our partners at Faber and Faber and the BBC, Dotti Irving, Liz Sich, Kate Wright-Morris, Truda Spruyt and Sophie Rochester at Colman Getty and, as ever, everyone at Forward.

William Sieghart

Foreword

POETRY KEEPS ON COMING. Between May and July 2005 my fellow judges and I read a total of about 7,000 poems. To put this another way – 19 poems are written every single day of the year, and those are just the ones that are considered publishable. We each read 116 books of this year's poems (77 were nominated for the Best Collection, 39 for the Best First Collection) and a further 107 poems nominated for Best Single Poem. For an annual harvest of poetry in Britain these are impressive figures; but are they evidence of creative abundance, of how much there is that needs to be said or just simply a glut of loquacity?

We read many good books, but at times when judging felt not only word weary but clobbered by bad poems. On occasion, we wondered what had happened to the famed slim volume of old, as collection after collection topped a hundred pages or a hundred poems or more. There are poetic Stakhanovites out there whose production levels rival Korean car manufacturers. Slow down, we wanted to say, throw away more, publish less. It was not only these books that seemed to be woefully under-edited. Many collections, short and long, dipped and faltered as poor poems or the same poem in different trousers crowded out stronger work. Some books left us wondering why the poet had opted for poetry rather than prose, or cooking even. This wasn't a good year overall for attention to metre, stress, rhythm or music. A rhyme is so rare these days that the few poets who do it well were greeted with a cheer around our judging table. What does this all add up to? After reading two or three bad books in a row, you can feel overcome by a sense of poetry being thought of as a right rather than an art. Shouldn't we be legislating against this, or at least policing those 19 poems a day more strongly?

Then a good book comes from the pile and all is well again. And this year we found much to cheer us and get excited about. To our first judging meeting in July we brought between us 19 books in the Best Collection category and 15 in the Best First Collection category that we thought worthy of discussion, shortlisting, prizewinning even. The day was a long one. The variety of possible winners showed not only the judges' wide interests, discrimination and preferences but also the richly varied voice of the best of the year's poetry.

We felt there were enough good books out this year to demand that those on our shortlist for the Best Collection prize had to be their author's best work to date. The five books, we feel, are this; several others came very close. The books on the shortlist for Best First Collection show maturity, confidence and originality enough to have several of us checking that these were indeed first books. Whilst these collections contained some excellent poems about childhood and early years – those staples of a first book – they were also doing new things that a poet of any age or publishing history would be proud of. The five Best Single Poem nominations offer a panorama of the widest territories of poetry and its concerns – beautiful close observation; surrealism; a sense of tradition both venerated and laughed at; current affairs intruding on the imagination; the richness of stories, places and times not our own.

But to gauge the prevailing tone of a year's poems is impossible. After reading 7,000 of them you can feel that everything has been said, but nothing has stuck. A few observations stand out. A tally I kept revealed three times as many poems about blackbirds – surely the nightingale of our time – as about the war in Iraq or 9/11. There were a couple of exceptional books, but otherwise the love poem seems a goner; but we were impressed by old and young poets making death's horrible and long-established truths tell vividly again and again. Nature hovers vaguely or trips you up depending on who you are reading, but is most defiantly here again as a legitimate subject. City life, briefly on its uppers in the greening of British poetry, is coming back strong with some strikingly original vocabularies and registers. There are even some jokes here. The best poems, as ever, tell you things you never knew you knew. Geoffrey Hill's difficult, bold and angry book, *Scenes From Comus*, offers an image of the poet today that captures the complexity of their job when he says 'call me fantasist lately assigned to reality'. We hope our 15 shortlisted poets show themselves well equipped for this work.

My great thanks to my fellow judges and their combination of quiet brilliance, perspicacity, left-field exasperation and trenchant close-reading: the literary editor of *The Guardian*, Claire Armitstead; the novelist Romesh Gunesekera and poets Maura Dooley and Michael Symmons Roberts. We were looked after with skill and kindness by Kate Wright-Morris of Colman Getty and William Sieghart at Forward deserves the thanks of all those involved or interested in poetry in Britain today.

Tim Dee, *July 2005*

Publisher acknowledgements

Moniza Alvi · How the Words Feared the Mouth · *How the Stone Found its Voice* · Bloodaxe Books

Iain Bamforth · Bucket · *A Place in the World* · Carcanet Press

Robin Behn · Inventory at Dusk · Poetry London

Kamau Brathwaite · Agoue · Wasifiri

Judy Brown · Loudness · Poetry News

Colette Bryce · Early Version · *The Full Indian Rope Trick* · Picador

Carmen Bugan · Fertile Ground · *Crossing the Carpathians* · Oxford Poets/Carcanet Press

John Burnside · The Good Neighbour · De Humani Corporis Fabrica · *The Good Neighbour* · Jonathan Cape

Matthew Caley · Lines Written Upon a Prophylactic Found in a Brixton Gutter · *The Scene of My Former Triumph* · Wrecking Ball Press

Carole Coates · Daughters · *The Goodbye Edition* · Shoestring Press

David Constantine · 'There is Nothing I Can Tell You' · *Collected Poems* · Bloodaxe Books

Robert Crawford · The Also Ran · London Review of Books

Tim Cumming · Punctuation · *The Rumour* · Stride

Julia Darling · A Short Manifesto For My City · *Apology for Absence* · Arc Publications

Mark Doty · Heaven For Paul · *School of the Arts* · Jonathan Cape

Carol Ann Duffy · Absence · *Rapture* · Picador

Paul Durcan · The Far Side of the Island · *The Art of Life* · Harvill Press

Helen Farish · Drifts · Programme · *Intimates* · Jonathan Cape

Paul Farley · Liverpool Disappears for a Billionth of a Second · The North

Jennie Feldman · Bonfire on the Beach · *The Lost Notebook* · Anvil Press

Alan Gillis · Don't You · *Somebody, Somewhere* · Gallery Books

Jane Griffiths · Clairvoyance · *Icarus on Earth* · Bloodaxe Books

Contents

Shortlisted Poems
The Forward Prize for Best Collection

John Burnside

THE GOOD NEIGHBOUR

Somewhere along this street, unknown to me,
behind a maze of apple trees and stars,
he rises in the small hours, finds a book
and settles at a window or a desk
to see the morning in, alone for once,
unnamed, unburdened, happy in himself.

I don't know who he is; I've never met him
walking to the fish-house, or the bank,
and yet I think of him, on nights like these,
waking alone in my own house, my other neighbours
quiet in their beds, like drowsing flies.

He watches what I watch, tastes what I taste:
on winter nights, the snow; in summer, sky.
He listens for the bird lines in the clouds
and, like that ghost companion in the old
explorers' tales, that phantom in the sleet,
fifth in a party of four, he's not quite there,
but not quite inexistent, nonetheless;

and when he lays his book down, checks the hour
and fills a kettle, something hooded stops,
as cell by cell, a heartbeat at a time,
my one good neighbour sets himself aside,
and alters into someone I have known:
a passing stranger on the road to grief,
husband and father; rich man; poor man; thief.

De Humani Corporis Fabrica
after Vesalius

I know the names of almost
nothing

      not the bone
between my elbow and my wrist
that sometimes aches
from breaking
        years ago

            and not
the plumb line
from the pelvis
to the knee

less ache than hum
        where
in my nineteenth year
a knife blade slit through nerves
and nicked a vein

leaving the wall intact
        the valves
still working
so the blood kept flooding out
till Eleanor
      a nurse on evening shift

opened the wound
and made me whole again.

I have no words
for chambers in the heart
the smaller bones
        the seat of gravity

or else I know the names
but not the function:
ganglia
      the mental foramen
the hypothalamus
        the duodenum.

Once
    in our old school library
             I took
a book down from the shelf
and opened it to stripped flesh
            and the cords
of muscle
     ribbed and charred
like something barbecued

the colours wrong
        the single eye exposed:
a window into primal emptiness.

I sat for hours
      amazed
        and horrified
as if I had been asked to paraphrase
this body with the body I possessed:
hydraulics for a soul
        cheese-wire for nerves
a ruff of butcher's meat
         in place of thought.

I've read how Michelangelo would buy
a stolen corpse
                    to study
                            in the dark
the movement of a joint
                        or how a face
articulates the workings of the heart

how Stubbs would peel
the cold hide from a horse
and peer into the dark machinery
of savage grace

but I have never learned
                        nor wished to learn
how bodies work
                other than when they move
and breathe
            corporis fabrica

is less to me than how a shudder starts
and runs along the arm
                        toward the wings
that flex and curl
between the shoulder blades

– so I will lie beside you here
                            unnamed
until my hands recover from your skin

a history of tides
                    a flock of birds
the love that answers love
                        when bodies meet

and map themselves anew
                                  cell after cell
touch after glancing touch
                                  the living flesh

revealing and erasing what it knows
on secret charts
                    of watermark
                              and vellum.

David Harsent

Baby Blue

She might be singing 'My buttie, my lolly, my blue-eyed boy'
as she stoops to take him up in joy,

then stops on a broken note, her own eyes full
as she catches a glimpse of the sky through the skull.

STREET SCENES

(i)
Two greybeards playing chess, would you believe,
their sweetwood table and chairs at one remove
from the corner of the crossroads, where a dove
drifts down through the trompe l'oeil clouds of a gable-
      end to LOVE
IS ALL YOU NEED and SNAJPER! One grips his sleeve
to wipe his nose; one threatens the knight's move.
The same crossroads where push has so often come to
      shove.

(ii)
Broken glass in the Street of Clocks
Empty coats in the Street of Spindles
In the Street of Bridegrooms, broken locks
Burning books in the Street of Candles

(iii)
If you look closely you can see what it is, but you do have to look
closely, what with the early-evening light skating on the slick
and coming back at you off puddles on the tarmac.
This would have been three hours or more after the attack,
everything lying heavy, everything seeming to own the trick
of stillness, that shopping trolley, for instance, the gutted truck,
and these: one face-down over there, one in the crook
of another's arm, one flat out, one heaped like an open book,
one caught on the turn, arms out like a stopped clock,
one leaning against a door, as if about to knock.
But that over there: look again: did you ever see the like?

(iv)
The 'Golden Couple of Ballroom' are dancing the alley-ways,
soft-shoeing amid the shrapnel, lost in each other's gaze.

(v)

Something going through, something much like a hound
or wolf, in the hour *entre chien et loup*, the blue
hour when birdsong stops, just for a minute or two,
and the dead in the graveyard shuffle up the queue.

Something lean and low-slung, its muzzle to the ground,
something leaving a drip-trail of blood or piss.
It has come by way of the rift and the pretty pass,
slipping between the dead cert and the near-miss.

Something that whines and whimpers, much like the sound
of a child in pain, or love's last gasp. It shows
a backbone like a hat-rack, an eye like a bruise,
in its mouth, a rib (is it?), dark meat, the pope's nose.

Alan Jenkins

Effects

I held her hand, that was always scarred
From chopping, slicing, from the knives that lay in wait
In bowls of washing-up, that was raw,
The knuckles reddened, rough from scrubbing hard
At saucepan, frying pan, cup and plate
And giving love the only way she knew,
In each cheap cut of meat, in roast and stew,
Old-fashioned food she cooked and we ate;
And I saw that they had taken off her rings,
The rings she'd kept once in her dressing-table drawer
With faded snapshots, long-forgotten things
(Scent-sprays, tortoise-shell combs, a snap or two
From the time we took a holiday 'abroad')
But lately had never been without, as if
She wanted everyone to know she was his wife
Only now that he was dead. And her watch? –
Classic ladies' model, gold strap – it was gone,
And I'd never known her not have *that* on,
Not in all the years they sat together
Watching soaps and game shows I'd disdain
And not when my turn came to cook for her,
Chops or chicken portions, English, bland,
Familiar flavours she said she preferred
To whatever 'funny foreign stuff'
Young people seemed to eat these days, she'd heard;
Not all the weeks I didn't come, when she sat
Night after night and stared unseeing at
The television, at her inner weather,
Heaved herself upright, blinked and poured
Drink after drink, and gulped and stared – the scotch
That, when he was alive, she wouldn't touch,
That was her way to be with him again;
Not later in the psychiatric ward,

Where she blinked unseeing at the wall, the nurses
(Who would steal anything, she said), and dreamt
Of when she was a girl, of the time before
I was born, or grew up and learned contempt,
While the TV in the corner blared
To drown some 'poor soul's' moans and curses,
And she took her pills and blinked and stared
As the others shuffled round, and drooled, and swore...
But now she lay here, a thick rubber band
With her name on it in smudged black ink was all she wore
On the hand I held, a blotched and crinkled hand
Whose fingers couldn't clasp mine any more
Or falteringly wave, or fumble at my sleeve –
The last words she had said were *Please don't leave*
But of course I left; now I was back, though she
Could not know that, or turn her face to see
A nurse bring the little bag of her effects to me.

HERITAGE

England, and a drive through farms,
through dripping lanes, bumper-deep in mud,
diseased herds suffering the weather
and pubs where couples drained their years together,
sitting with pursed lips and crossed arms
over pints of bitter and tomato juice,
and me chewing my own bitter cud,
and me logging all of it for future use

in some piece of versified revenge
as we joined the tailback past Stonehenge
and Salisbury, past Keep Out signs
and mile on mile of razor-wire,
past the prehistoric mines
and dug-outs, fox-holes, shelling-scars,
past the skyward-pointing spire
and mile on mile of oncoming cars;

just to drift through panelled rooms, past walls
of flushed, same-featured faces
or wander round some flowering oasis
while I, stiff from the drive down, bored
half to death, hung-over, sour with guilt
imagined my hard-earned reward:
her cupped hand on my tightened balls,
her legs parting slyly under the B&B's damp quilt...

*

The paths we trudged through Somethingshire!
And once she said, out of the blue
if we couldn't talk, if all we could share
was time, there wasn't any point in going on –
bad enough, but the bigger scare

(this stopped me in my tracks, it's true)
was waiting by the twisted tree
I ducked behind to answer – as did she –

that 'call of nature' (from the beer):
a cow's skull, grinning. *Soon you will be gone,*
it said; *what can you share but this,*
but time, your moment here? Which will pass,
as fleeting as the pause before a wave,
as your footsteps on this grass
which might be covering your grave.
Caught short, you are nothing, piss

and wind, a shrunken cock, the Kleenex-scrap
she wipes herself with, that is whipped into the void –
as you will be. (She hoiked up her pants,
I mimed absorption in some guidebook crap...)
This is no myth, no chivalric romance:
you won't sit for ever in the dappled shade
of oak and beech, such as you once enjoyed;
you won't be reborn, you'll dwindle, fade

and disappear, become your names
illegible on a lichen-covered headstone
in some forgotten churchyard, overgrown
with weeds and briars and brambles
or go to ash, to smoke and air
inbreathed by nature-lovers on their rambles –
who will watch you slide into the flames
and shed a shy, a shuddering tear?

No silent gratitude in Georgian rooms
(Family Solicitors, Commissioners for Oaths),
no deeds of trust, no much-loved homes,
no legacy of life, no precious heirlooms –
what good are they without a sodding heir? –

just a few hundred well-thumbed 'tomes',
a thrift-shop rack of stale-smelling clothes,
some letters tied with ribbon, 'Dear –'...

*

Breakfast: while she watched her eggs congeal
I contemplated circumcised remains
of sausage, and a bacon-rind;
an hour before, I'd fucked her from behind
and now her face wore all the strain
of wanting not to punish me,
of battling indecisively
some hurt of mine she could not heal...

Back, then, through half-timbered towns,
past the homes of billionaires
who long ago cashed in their shares
and bought England, whose slim blonde wives
work out and punish four-wheel-drives
on their way to an assignation
over lunch in the hotel lounge, 'The Downs';
past the theme-park (Heritage Nation)

where the beer-bellies, shaven heads
and shiny shell-suits swarm
over litter-strewn lawns, and storm
the Bouncy Castle and the potting sheds
'Now selling lager, lolly's, video's';
past the lane that every flasher knows;
past the woods where little girls take root.
And none of this would bear fruit.

Alice Oswald

Moon Hymn

I will give you one glimpse
a glimpse of the moon's grievance
whose appearance is all pocks and points
that look like frost-glints

I will wave my hand to her
in her first quarter
when the whole world is against her
shadowy exposure of her centre

o the moon loves to wander
I will go clockwise and stare
when she is huge when she is half elsewhere
half naked, in struggle with the air

and growing rounder and rounder
a pert peering creature
I love her sidling and awkward
when she's not quite circular

o criminal and ingrown
skinned animal o moon
carrying inside yourself your own
death's head, your dark one

why do you chop yourself away
piece by piece, to that final trace
of an outline of ice
on a cupful of space?

Various Portents

Various stars. Various kings.
Various sunsets, signs, cursory insights.
Many minute attentions, many knowledgeable watchers,
Much cold, much overbearing darkness.

Various long midwinter Glooms.
Various Solitary and Terrible Stars.
Many Frosty Nights, many previously Unseen
    Sky-flowers.
Many people setting out (some of them kings) all clutching at
    stars.

More than one North Star, more than one South Star.
Several billion elliptical galaxies, bubble nebulae, binary systems,
Various dust lanes, various routes through varying thicknesses of
    Dark,
Many tunnels into deep space, minds going back and forth.

Many visions, many digitally enhanced heavens,
All kinds of glistenings being gathered into telescopes:
Fireworks, gasworks, white-streaked works of Dusk,
Works of wonder and/or water, snowflakes, stars of frost...

Various dazed astronomers dilating their eyes,
Various astronauts setting out into laughterless earthlessness,
Various 5,000-year-old moon maps,
Various blindmen feeling across the heavens in braille.

Various gods making beautiful works in bronze,
Brooches, crowns, triangles, cups and chains,
And all sorts of drystone stars put together without mortar.
Many Wisemen remarking the irregular weather.

Many exile energies, many low-voiced followers,
Watchers of wisps of various glowing spindles,
Soothsayers, hunters in the High Country of the Zodiac,
Seafarers tossing, tied to a star...

Various people coming home (some of them kings). Various
  headlights.
Two or three children standing or sitting on the low wall.
Various winds, the Sea Wind, the sound-laden Winds of Evening
Blowing the stars towards them, bringing snow.

John Stammers

Fancy Man

Usually I'm handsome.
I am the well-dressed man who arrives first at dinner parties
and is taking a turn alone around the garden when you arrive.
Lingering at the edge of discussions of social mores,
I express orthogonal opinions over the braised guinea fowl
such as that 'the sex act' is overrated
whereas *conversation* is the most provocative of possible contacts.
My pursuit or occupation is often in the Arts.
Women ask me to talk about my work
and say to their spouses on the way home, 'He's *so* interesting';
they get home faster that way.
Their hubbies fuck them hard that night;
it is uncertain that they like it.
Tell a good joke, slap a good back,
shake a strong hand (the palm slightly turned over theirs).
What's past is most of the things: cocktail bars, ocean liners,
the marginal traffics that call for a nice take on the scope of the
    lawful.
I have fired a gun,
been threatened at knife-point and felt its tip on my face.
There are cut flowers in my living room.
Sunday afternoons it's the supermarket
for pre-prepared cuisine such as smoked salmon roulade or
    bruschetta,
full-bodied red wines and the meal-in-a-bag.
My cleaning lady tells me to 'never mind' because 'hope springs!'
Known former girlfriends are young and decorous

and leak sad little tears
when I split up with them 'For *you*, darling, not for me'.
I am still *there* for them
and buy them smart lunches on their birthdays.
Secret loves have been long-time married, had kids.
'He *does* love me,' they tell me.
But that's not love, just a settled form of hate.
They sing out into the air when *we* make love.
In photographs in Sunday magazines
of contemporary buildings and galleries
there is always a room that I am in.
I am there looking out at you in sunglasses.
I stand in the shadows so that you cannot fully see me.
Someone did something to me once
and I have never forgiven everybody.

Ask Them

Ask them all where it is hid;
ask the old man and the kid,
fortune tellers in their stripy tents,
circus artists, governments,
cyclists round the velodromes,
Rosicrucians, garden gnomes.
Enquire politely of city women in their fashion heels;
ask the sturgeons, lampreys and the conger eels.
Go to Lourdes, Delphi, London Zoo;
lobby wolverine and kangaroo.
Humbly petition the Arapaho
(if it were known, surely they would know).
Look in each house, each studio flat;
pray to God from Mt Ararat.
Ask them, ask them every one;
examine the poles, go to the sun.
You will not find a single clue;
it is no longer there for you.

Shortlisted Poems
The Felix Dennis Prize for Best First Collection

Helen Farish

Drifts

I've always been able to turn over in bed
to the right or to the left and not feel
my breasts' rearrangement. They are snow,
drifts shaping and reshaping in the night.
It must be thirty years since they settled
on my chest, making themselves
at home. Now I stop myself turning
either way for the pain. I hold them and ask
what the matter is. I apologise for taking
each snowflake for granted. I say I will learn
to live in the world as I used to
when my chest was flat. If it snowed
I couldn't settle until I was out there,
moulding it.

PROGRAMME

She loves the radio, the freedom it gives
to listen out the back or as she's passing to and fro
or sitting in the half-house half-garden room

on a midsummer's Sunday evening
listening to a three-hour programme on the monsoon,
and the front door is open and the back,

and every now and then the setting light
coming past the lavender she's recently started caring for
and the honeysuckle she never used to notice nor those roses

hidden till she chopped back the buddleia – the light
coming past the flowering jasmine and the hanging basket
she's so pleased with stops her,

makes her see how much of her life
has been lived in this house,
that she's become who she is here

and what she will remember of these years is not
the times when living alone seemed a problem to solve
but the peace:

looking at a house she has done her best in,
loving small successes, the hanging basket, the picture in the half-
house half-garden room, that repotted plant,

and her larger successes – allowing herself the pleasure
of a three-hour programme on the monsoon
sorting through a box of postcards with a green glass of gin,

seeing all those places she's been to: but her journey
to this programme, her swept front path, this is
the one she's most proud of.

Nick Laird

THE LAYERED

doubt

Empty Laird was called that 'cause
his Christian name was Matthew
and his middle one was Thomas.

Towards the end he commented
that by his-self he'd made a sixth
of the disciples, and forgone a life

on the quest for the rest.
And a good book.
Or a decent cause.

fear

Laird Jnr was a tyke, a terrier.

A nit-picker who grew to a hair-splitter,
he was not so much scared of his shadow,
as of its absence. He knew he was see-thru.

It was a very modern kind of terror.

lust

the one   who went on to become   Mrs Laird
the wife   walked into my life
one night   I'd had six or seven pints

and it was either that or fight

she was just the type   I like
chest spilling out of itself   slender-hipped
with a Nubian face closed to the public
waist   my exact hand-span

poised and filmic   she was drinking my usual
unthinkable and very
very do-able   I am not a good man
into my grave into my grave into my grave she was laid

POETRY

It's a bit like looking through the big window
on the top deck of the number 47.

I'm watching you, and her, and all of them,
but through my own reflection.

Or opening my eyes when everyone's praying.
The wave machine of my father's breathing,

my mother's limestone-fingered steeple,
my sister's tiny fidgets, and me, moon-eyed, unforgetting.

And then the oak doors flapping slowly open to let us out,
like some great injured bird trying to take flight.

Richard Price

from A Spelthorne Bird List

Coot

The coot was a pint of stout. It slipped out from The Ferry during a fight. Mathematically white, it was plunged by its beak in mathematical black. To uppity swans it does not signify. The same goes for Joe Duck.

Heron

A greying Senior Lecturer in Fish Studies (Thames Valley), he stands in frozen hop concentration, regarding a lectern only he can see. Still, he gets results. He's hoping for a chair.

Kingfisher

Blue. I mean green. Blue, green.   Gone.

from HANDHELD

The world is busy, Katie

The world is busy, Katie, and tonight
the planes are playing, fine, alright, but soon
the folk behind those blinks will nap, sleep tight,
as you will too, beneath a nitelite moon.
The world is busy, Katie, but it's late –
the trains are packing up, the drunks are calm.
The fast, the slow, has gone. It's only freight
that storms the garage lane. It means no harm.
The world is busy, Katie, but it's dark –
the lorries nod, they snort, they spoil their chrome.
They hate to be alone. For them, a lay-by's home.
The world is busy, Katie, like I said,
but *you're* the world – and tired. It's time for bed.

The grip

People will not love you
when we are dead.

A woman in a bib
saying nothing in screeches,
whose grip and spit and sleeplessness
lack all endearment,
though you have been
dear enough to us,
can only hope for what is yet
termed a home,

but it's some consolation
you understand nothing
of nuance, nor the future.

James Sheard

from Eva's Homecoming
Neuer Wall (ehm. Dreckwall) *
    (Exhibit Label, Museum of Hamburg History)

When I moored up
against the hulk of Hamburg,
gulls rose
on the cries of shiphands.

Bismarck bowed his head.

Overnight, the wind
had fought the light a little.
Thin cloud had made a petal of the moon,
laid scales on the sea's grey hide.

It failed to rise. It failed
to shake me loose.

Last night, a woman walked
in the night ship's diesel hum,
her cotton shift trailing soiled
over dusty feet. The nub
of each outer toe lifted
to sail above the decks.

I saw her then in Baltic furs,
bristling with vanillas.

I saw her, too, as Eva,
now twenty years dead.

* *New Dyke (formerly Crap Dyke)*

I carry Eva's ashes –

Poor Eva's ashes.
Eva's muttering, restless ashes.
Eva's fucking ashes.
Those fucking ashes of Eva's –

I carry Eva's ashes
to the landing-bridges.

What's treulos, *Schatz?*
Faithless? Feckless?
Untrue? *Ja,*
all those.

HOTEL MASTBOSCH

Old money smells of civet, folds in
and whispers *scurf* and *scrofula*.
Its women oil pearls at nutmeg throats,
sure-fingered as a Chinese tallyman
clicking behind a carved Sumatran screen.

There are flickers of acknowledgement,
eyes with the tilt and swivel of loose rivets,
noses which lift and flare
above whole vanished islands of spice.

And then the sounds of shunting-yards,
chased silver bracelets clanking down
on varnished tables, the huffy dismissals
of steam trains settling.

    The evening thickens
to a brown frottage of old wallpaper,
sticky with molasses, pressed tobacco,
the renderings of shelled insects.

Above it all,
the slap of leather and brass:
a trundle turning fans as if in Java,
cooling old fevers
and the orange of their bones.

Jane Yeh

CORRESPONDENCE

I've gotten nothing for weeks. You might think of me

As dated in a blue housecoat, buttoning and unbuttoning,
Waiting you out: I have my ways

Of keeping time. When your letter comes, dogs will bark
Up and down the street. The tomatoes in the garden

Will explode like fireworks. Each day the mailman passes
In a reverie, illiterate, another cobweb

Grows across the door. Picture me
Going bald one hair at a time, combing and curling, burning

My hand on the iron once every hour: I like to
Keep myself busy. When I hear from you, *aurora*

Borealis will sweep across the sky. Every lottery ticket in my drawer
Will win. Even the mailman will know the letters

Of your name. If you bothered to notice, you would see me
Turning to gold rather slowly, bone

By bone, the way teeth come
Loose from the gums, the way animals go

Extinct, in geological time.

Self-Portrait After Vermeer

Already I am too old, coming to
An appointment 7,417 days late, penitent

In pearls and homespun, high-waisted, tied up
With muslin: an Old Master. I've got to break

For it and believe
There is another way, that curtains can be drawn

Over windows, voracious
Dreams; somehow

To count slow enough
Under my breath to go

Unseen. I am crouching behind you,
Trying to shrink and failing

Fast. But in this kind of divine
Light I am transfigurable, re-

Formed, chimærical. There are those who doubt
And those who wait. I will keep coming

Late, playing my age, framing myself
While you steal a little here and now.

Shortlisted Poems
The Forward Prize for Best Single Poem
in memory of Michael Donaghy

Paul Farley

LIVERPOOL DISAPPEARS FOR A BILLIONTH OF A SECOND

Shorter than the blink inside a blink
the National Grid will sometimes make, when you'll
turn to a room and say: Was that just me?

People sitting down for dinner don't feel
their chairs taken away/put back again
much faster than that trick with tablecloths.

A train entering the Olive Mount cutting
shudders, but not a single passenger
complains when it pulls in almost on time.

The birds feel it, though, and if you see
starlings in shoal, seagulls abandoning
cathedral ledges, or a mob of pigeons

lifting from a square as at gunfire,
be warned, it may be happening, but then
those sensitive to bat-squeak in the backs

of necks, who claim to hear the distant roar
of comets on the turn – these may well smile
at a world restored, in one piece; though each place

where mineral Liverpool goes wouldn't believe
what hit it: all that sandstone out to sea
or meshed into the quarters of Cologne.

I've felt it a few times when I've gone home,
if anything, more often now I'm old,
and the gaps between get shorter all the time.

Stephen Knight

99 POEMS
i. m.

A face that, though in shadow, still appears
A graceful Child, his father's joy!
A ship-wrack on his bed, night being past
Abandoned by day in a pinkish lounge, his final
ahv naebawdy
'Alas!' quaþ he, 'now me is wo
Almost as true as his kindness, I'll say, almost as true as his
    laughter, his labored jokes
Ane faiding flour, away as wind it weiris
Angled to face each other
Are you to leave like this

Before you say
Below this faultless Stone, is laid
Bid mountain-light attend your bower
Brimmer Street irregular! Father's barbarous dress-sword

Carriages, clergymen, unsmiling faces, delicate hands
Cold rivers, colder seas, alas

Death's oompah band

'E weren't no bloomin' 'ero, all 'e did was live an' die
Empire State patrician

Fare-thee-well, o glaikit man
Farewel, more lov'd than any I recal
Father! how soon this night o'er-brims the trees
Fog after dusk, murmuring small requests
Fold the sky in half, shake out the stars
For he is affraid
fus ting dat crazy clack

Go, finde a Store of Tears among the Clouds
God of all things, all things rain and air, all flying things

He gave his Checks – the Whistle blew
He Rambld Ere The Mornings Dews Could Flee
He visited the loft, not long before
He was withouten any peere
He woke again last night, and cried
Here he sat, his face o'ershadowed
Here rests a gentle Man, whose modest Heart
Here shall be rest for evermo
His dreaming eyes, his brow in touch
His hat still on its peg. His shoes lined up
His watch-face like a skating rink
How still the moon-blanch'd sea
'How's the Humber? How's the wife? Do you remember Lilian?'

I dreamed you stood alone, in No Man's Land
I have seen Him in a meagre light
I sought, ô grassie mountaines, thy constant fellowship
I THOUGHT of Thee, unfathomable one
I took no part
Icy nim-air, a barn done Dinner Street
If Death, growne wearie of his warres
Il laisse tomber son modelling knife, *tant pis, tant pis*

Lately, I have seen the fellow with his pockets inside out
Lethean foam-flowers rise from the sewers
Like as a winde that fadeth ere blacke night
Lost in the pea-drills behind our house
LOVE NAILS   TriBeCa Nails   (too much

May his comfy shoes, O Lord
Mr Chips, Bulk Catering
My dreams of thee! How soon the morning comes!
My father had heard tell
My father picked up a stone
My latest thoughts return to thee

[…] nis þer no niȝte
Niver say tha'rt frit o' me
No murmur stirs your room, tonight, no voices call below
No nothin kin explain it, yes indeedy
No winde there blew, the skie was bare of anie bird

O thou whose falt'ring hand the waters tune
O turn thy Waters through my Heart
Oh, sweet was the rain as it fell on Swiss Cottage
Once my Lamentation was an envied horror

Plip plop plip

Sisyphus, your heart
Snow in the branches, where birds perch still as graves
Stars observe, with their flat blank eyes
Sythen in that spote hit fro me sprange

That was a crappy bookstore smell, *jeez*. Old guys
The fields of snow did breathe
The laundromat is crowded. Every ghost
The sea it was brazen and icy
The Show'r come down on Tory and Whig, Dust gone to Mud
The stairs became more difficult
Thy Exile from this World, deare Friend
Thy Publick Virtue, Father, all attest
'Tis three years since, his grave is bare

Uh-oh

Vnmesurable greiff, Alas! how straunge is this
Voices on the wireless

We are becoming
Weepe with me, to night, all hope is over-come
Well, then! Let no man disapprove
When first your slender breath
When the evenèn wind do blow vrom zight
Where rootless poppies lie
Who could not stay a while

Yf all my wordes were raine upon thy grave
Yonder
You could not face me, then
You could not speak, nor even smile, before you turned
You cupped one hand to catch the crumbs
Your hands

Sarah Maguire

PASSAGES

Decree: clear skies
over the heart
of London: cirrus

nothing less
flaming
the far edge of blueness,

nothing less
marking
the absolute boundaries

of air, of resolution.
A cast of slowing jumbos,
emptied of fuel, begins

the descent:
trawling
the long southern flight path

down into Heathrow.
When the huge wheels
hatch

from that cold,
aluminium belly,
will a petrified figure

plummet down
(this time)
into a carpark,

breath frozen midair,
the wrapt human form
seared

on the landing gear
tossed three miles clear
from touchdown

from migration?
The big silvered craft
run the gamut of light,

taking in evening
buoyant, journeyed:
pushed to the edge

of the city: now exposed,
with its parcel of lights,
its human freight

inching homewards
through dusk, mid-September,
as fear

slips its cold roots
through the known.
The dull muddied Thames

is full of the equinox,
dragged by the moon
the dun waters

flush to the Barrier:
a ruined city checked,
a whole rumoured ocean

balanced in abeyance.
Tides dissolve memory:
history

loosens its cargoes
into the tides
promiscuously mingling,

forgetting,
heading out to the open.
But the silt sifts on,

turning and sorting:
as the docklands fall
out of sight,

cargoless,
trafficless, winches abandoned,
ceilings stove in

to the skies.
And the skies are rivers
freighting

the burdens
of rivers: transhumance
precious and raw

now landing on tarmac.
The jets tick
as they cool,

boxes contracting
on earth,
as rivets ease back:

the hulk
emptied of passengers
now filling

with migrants:
labouring in the site
of exile and arrival.

The swallows
left weeks ago,
with no notice:

one afternoon
the skies
were abandoned:

lack
takes them southwards.
And in the formal garden,

the last hybrid roses
flare rose-pink and
salmon and mauve,

but the sap's on the turn.
And the earth is balanced,
day equaling night:

and is equally
unbalanced
as rumours are pieced

into news.
After this: winter.
The youngest vixen repeats

her sharp scent,
doubles back, excited
back again,

crouching,
back now to the rough path:
slips

under the light paling fence
and is
gone:

Katherine Pierpoint

BUFFALO CALF

A buffalo calf, beautiful, lies asleep under the water-tap.
A calf, bright oil-drum black, blissful, at hot roost,
front legs folded in the shitty mud,
and eyes rolled back,
smiling hugely –
he's a deformed fairy,
or drugged, ecstatic dragon, landed half-on, half-in the earth.

Dripped on,
he sucks, eyes shut, all day, on that one sensation.

A slow, kohl-eyed cow walks by, to her daily fieldwork in the rice,
but dressed in the tassels, paint, and tin bells of a dancer –
she's made more beautiful each moment through her movement.

A temple elephant too. The surprise of it – in town! at *church*! –
for an elephant is its own cathedral.
Even thinking of an elephant
is architecture, elaborate; a plain hugeness at first disguising the
    subtleties there;
and there it stands and stands, and stands, at the busy temple gate,
little as a lap-dog
against the mounting pyramid of stones,
the mass of carvings, the unending, up-ending sex,
the linked aeons of miracles.

Polka-dot flowers and river deltas chalked across her steep forehead,
as if bringing out her private depths and cliffs of thought,
the bright hibiscus in there, the mudfields, long bathes;
and she sways, bored, bored, bored,
leaning this way and that against the air.

Peter Scupham

SEVENTY YEARS A SHOWMAN
('Lord' George Sanger grows up)

1833, Oxford. Hilton's drivers try to pass Wombwell's:
a clash of crowbars, tent-poles, whips. *The fat man*
made for the living skeleton with a door hook;
the skeleton batters the fat man with a peg mallet.
Wombwell's elephants break their wagon to splinters
while *two little trembling figures, in our night-gowns,*
press at their caravan windows. It goes down blazing.

At six years old, he works the family peepshow,
a mite *in a clean pinafore and well-greased boots*
pattering the death of Maria Marten by William Corder
in the famous Red Barn. At twenty-six peepholes
strings tighten on Corder's neck by tallow candlelight;
at the Red Lion, Wantage, a wretch with a fagging-hook
half-severs the landlady's head. *All was confusion.*

Learn the moral. *Keep your temper, my boys,*
keep your temper. The peep-show is briskly altered:
a cut-up woman, taproom, savage sickleman – *and with*
a plentiful supply of carmine for gore, the trick was done.
Newbury is all smallpox, bells and funerals. Father
lances each child's arm with a darning needle, rubs in
pustular serum. *The results were all that could be wished,*

and winter-work is carrying goods round Berkshire.
At the 'Bell and Bottle', two strangers beg a lift, hoist
a parcel of duds and things for a little job on the back rail.
He loosens the sack, and glimpses, bared by moonlight,
the pallid wax-like face of a dead woman. Trembling,
he gives way, drops off the wagon, runs to catch it up –
Georgie, not a word! Keep on by the side of the horses!

Watching his passengers drowse off, Father pulls up
by a fellow wagoner whose boy races for assistance,
then cracks on into a mob *armed with pitchforks, cudgels,
and other rustic weapons* who haul away the bodysnatchers.
Next summer, Father's blunderbuss guards the caravan
while thirty thousand Chartists tramp by to sack Newport.
When twenty-four soldiers drop the leaders by musket-fire

'*The Riots at Newport*' quickly revamps the peepshow,
but at Lansdown Fair Bath roughs led by Carroty Kate –
strong as a navvy, a big brutal animal – wreck the booths
in a frenzy of drink, fire and mayhem. The showmen
yoke the wreckers on tent-ropes, drag them through water,
trice them to wheels, thrash them with whalebone whips:
Three dozen for every man jack of 'em. Lay on, boys!

On Romney Marsh, he slips on a roundabout. *A bolt
literally tore the flesh of the calf away from the limb.*
Father, who fought with Nelson on the Victory,
saddles up the horse, rides three miles for a doctor,
refuses amputation, sews back the calf, sailor-fashion –
sixteen huge stitches looping the silk. *Don't halloa,
it'll soon be finished! Be a man, Georgie!*

Glad when Nellie gives up *the Lion Queen business*,
he's off to Stalybridge wakes, where a row breaks out
at the gingerbread stall. Sheppard is kicked to pulp:
a ghastly shapeless thing in the clear sunlight,
purple stains blotching the white road-dust.
(Lancashire fights with teeth and iron-tipped clogs.)
That same night the family hear of Father's death,

and in the fall of the year he marries his Nellie.
Life is good with the *Wonderful Performing Fish*,
the *Tame Oyster* and the *Suspension by Ether*.
He performs in a charnel house, buys Astley's,
receives a gold medal from the Ostend Burgomaster,
tricks the Prince of Wales with a whitewashed elephant –
and is murdered in 1911 by a berserk servant.

Highly Commended Poems

2005

Moniza Alvi

How the Words Feared the Mouth

Some words lay quietly,
they didn't wish to be roused,

while others were restless,
waiting for the drama to begin.

Sensitive words feared the mouth –
that slash in the face, the hole

which could fill with potatoes and beer.
Half-formed words were often lost.

And others were equally unfortunate –
it was their fate

to be cruelly nailed to the air.

Iain Bamforth

A bucket stands collecting rain.
Blunt container, it collects
essence of only ocean
above some dun African savannah.
Capsizer of your head
should you try to plumb it.

It irons a puddle; no wider
wetness than its expanding sense:
matter as a meaning
steadily, irreversibly filling
something (say it bucket, say it)
at the bottom of its need.

All night, a lake lies shocked
above a bucket's tegument. Rain
spites its face. This red morning
foliage brightens the rim,
and hope is such a terrible violence
you, rider, hedge your bets.

Robin Behn

INVENTORY AT DUSK

One dark blue hospital gown
whose necklace of snaps shone
like a tiny constellation.

One vase of pussywillows
and another of long-stemmed swabs'
soft buds aswarm in contemplation.

Slumberous music, cello
(although he played piano). So,
one well-intended notion.

The small TV turned off
so there's a frame around the dark.
Plenteous devotions.

So at first I was not needed.
I knelt under the sky blue sky
of the lips, and traced the final motion

where the hand had curled
like a fern re-furled
to its first consecration.

What could I say to you, loose soul,
my confidant, new orphan,
shy of brash contrition?

The window stayed closed.
It wanted that, the soul.
Still stubborn about asking for directions.

I stroked its ether hair.
It stroked – the air.
And I sang. Not to my companion,

who is what singing is.
I sang to my father's not-knowing,
(the soul was already going)

I sang for his wild mouth.
I sang instead of truth.
I sang for a place to lean on.

And opened the window then.
A little. I did. But first I combed his hair
like going over the ocean.

Kamau Brathwaite

AGOUE

a sequence for
VOICE . CHORAL CHORUS . MUSIC & VODOUNISTAS
the music is im brooks . the vision is temne callender . the painting gérard valsin

*

first there is this frost and it was light

blue almost white
like cloud. icing of furushima
and then it was real cloud. like the blue

mountains

and then there are two loaves
of land. brown. w/straight
lines in them. running up out of the dark

water

and these loaves are a distant ilannn
like humps of a brontosaurus. w/out its head
or tail. sailing into the true

water

and the water is serene like peace and make a straight
line like anguilla
like ink under that scaly island

and there is the faintest breath of wind
upon these waters
so that it make no waves

only a gentile heave
or heaven where there would be fry
or shrimp or louvres
•

and then the fish

jump
-silver. w/red torch-
light eyes . the fins shining like steel terraces

or lovers

out of the palm trees green

and then the seven
-brothers of the rain-
bow . also

fish

jump straight up . in the air

two

from the one

three

one

-from the x-
act other

and in the royal centre
of the purple
tuning now softly to light

-in-
digo blue
dissolve of the darkness of blue

are the four

-w/ leopard stops and scissor-
-tails all-
-most in air. all-

most in water
brothers flying from branches to irie
. and as they fly .

whale & sirène

. not flying . not falling .
but like flow
-ing-
-flow-
-ing-
-flow-
-ing-

Judy Brown

LOUDNESS

After bad news, and its pulled-back fist,
flows in a sound that's not a sound. It's not
the brain's tide beating blood in propped
and shored-up workings, not the tapestried
texture of attended silence, the goffering
of quiet air folding and unfolding
        in a house where nothing is happening.

After bad news, you tell the seconds,
hungry for the hurrying thunder
that never comes. Instead a chemical fizz
fills the ears, before the descaling. An angel
rides the stirrup and anvil, spurring on the drum,
works like wild weather in wet sheets,
        flapping and cracking the body's flat muscles.

Long after the bad news, when it's bedded in,
you notice most clearly the mild loudness
of the not-so-old man in the foot tunnel,
drumming and drumming and biting his mouth.
The posed coins in his blue cloth
        are tiny, like a cast handful of earbones.

Colette Bryce

Our boat was slow to reach Bethsaida; winds oppressed us,
fast and cold, our hands were blistered from the oars.
We'd done to death our songs and jokes, with miles
to go, when Jesus spoke:

he said he'd crouched upon the shore, alone, engaged
in silent prayer, when, looking down, he started –
saw his own image crouching there. And when he leant
and dipped his hand

he swore he felt the fingers touch, and as he rose
the image stood and, slowly, each put out a foot
and took a step, and where they met, the weight of one
annulled the other;

then how he'd moved across the lake, walked on the soles
of his liquid self, and he described how cool it felt
on his aching, dusty feet; the way he'd strode a steady
course to board the boat

where we now sat – mesmerized. He gestured out
towards the shore, along the lake, then to himself,
and asked us all to visualize, to open what he always
called our 'fettered minds'.

Carmen Bugan

Fertile Ground

I was pruning tomato plants when they came to search
For weapons in our garden;
They dug the earth under the chickens, bell peppers,
Tiny melons, dill, and horseradishes.

I cried over sliced eggplants
Made one with the dirt,
Over fresh-dug earth and morning glories.

Their shovels uncovered bottles
With rusted metal caps – sunflower cooking oil
My father kept for 'dark days', purchased in days equally dark.
Their eyes lit – everyone got a bottle or two –
A promise for their families' meals.

And when the oil spilled on the ground, shiny over crushed
   tomatoes
They asked me about weapons we might have kept.
'Oil,' I said: 'You eat and live.
This alone makes one dangerous.'

Matthew Caley

LINES WRITTEN UPON A PROPHYLACTIC FOUND
IN A BRIXTON GUTTER

O useless balloon, supine, not the colour of dolor
but see-thru, salmon-pink, plugged with your load of ore
draped in the grating side by side
with imploded pizza-stars and half a crepe.

Squished jellyfish of desire, trodden under the fly-boy trainers
of crack-dealers by the Taxi-rank and noodle-bar
– witness to a union of souls or alleyway tremble –
spermicidal eel, you know the perfidious trade-routes,

how the underground waters of the Effra
distabilise our feet, how pomegranate or melon-seeds
from the glass-arcades stuck in the tread of our boots

might spring up a rash of fruit trees in the inner city
sometime and knowing also how joy is brief [and rarely
                         sanctioned by the Pontiff]
you dangle-drop, precariously, swim out for the open sea.

Carole Coates

DAUGHTERS

My daughter looks in the glass.
She's trying to find a face
that isn't mine.

When I'm not watching her
my mother turns grandmother –
sighs on the stair.

Their spine aches in my back
arching towards the hunch
I've already seen twice.

My flash daughter wears
my grandmother's feet,
speaks with my voice.

She'll lighten her hair
and redden her lips –
all the brightness to learn.

I check the colour of my eyes –
not green enough yet.
Colours must drain

flesh dwindle to bone
become porous with pain,
fragment in air.

My grandmother's skull –
I wrapped it in wool,
held it in my arms.

David Constantine

'THERE IS NOTHING I CAN TELL YOU...'

There is nothing I can tell you about the sea.

That it can't keep still and even in daylight
Is under the moon and host
To headlong wanderings and hunger
And that for its appearance it mates with the winds
In all their degrees and every glance of light...

And about islands there is nothing I can tell you.

The rush of landing – Where will we sleep tonight? –
And the selfsame evening, housed,
We climb to another Top Rock or Watch Hill –
Where tomorrow? And the little ferry
Will drag us away with samphire on our fingers...

There is nothing I can tell you about the sea and about the
    islands.

That they make us liable to the moon
Even to the starving wisp of her in daylight
And nervously alert to every start of water
And our fingers itchy for the herbs that do not grow inland
Night after night, deny it, you told me.

Robert Crawford

THE ALSO RAN

The hare wasn't there. The hare was nowhere
To be seen, a sheen
Of kicked-up dust, the hare's coat,
Every hair of the flank of the hare so sleek, so chic,
It was sponsored, it caressed his physique.
Out of sight, out of mind, the unsponsored tortoise fell
Into a vertical sleep that sank him deep
Down in his shell. He dreamed. He smelled the smell
Of formula one. The stop, start
Of his own heart slowed on the chicaned road
To hibernation. He dreamed station
After station flew past the filmy blue
Carriage window of dwam, his shell a bullet train
Trained to hurtle, to startle, but with tortoise feet,
Not wheels, not rails making the beat,
Beat, beat of speed. He felt torque eat
All of him, call to him, willing him, through him
Birling the earth. A surge, a rebirth
Hurried him on. Each hour, each day
Rushed further away. As he slept, stock still,
Every path, track, hill, housing estate, landfill
Site, every dawn, noon, night
Shot past faster, a happy disaster, a true
Gift of the gods, a one-off, out of the blue,
Till waving children, doe-eyed does, sped past
Ahead of sound, and the tortoise thought earth might
Out-accelerate light, the planet's race, pace, place
In the universe changing. Then, ranging
Further than any dream has ever gone,
The tortoise shone. A comet. A meteor. Shone,
His shell a re-entering rocket, a capsule straight down like a stone
From outer peace. Och, plunged in the innermost space
Of the dream, he was sure he had lost, and so sure he had won

In his way, and would have his day, the Spring Day
Of the Slow Start. He played his part
Well. He sang his dream and in the spring its claim
On his listeners grew. They knew, like you
And I, it was true.
Even the hares, when they heard what he said, stopped dead
Inside themselves, beside themselves, stunned
At how the tortoise seemed to have gunned, to have shot
From the starter's pistol by staying stock still. They thought
It was great, it was cool. They loved
How he hadn't moved but the earth had sped beneath him.
They were with him. When he sang, they sang along,
Whiskering, whistling his song. And the tortoise, sleepy, wiser,
Let them sing. And the hare? He was nowhere. A survivor
Off in a puff of dust, but in the huff
That sharper, tougher, fitter, leaner, thinner,
He was only the winner.

Tim Cumming

PUNCTUATION

It was the month her teeth came through,
the first words sinking their foundations.
I'd wake in the night, dream images billowing
like air bags, the brass plate of a hangover
bolted against my temple.
You couldn't believe the detail.
I'd go to her room
and pick her up, hold
her against my chest as she cried.
You didn't ever stop getting nearer,
you just kept on going off the paper,
scattering the room with punctuation.
Commas, colons, dashes. Stops.
They ran through you like blood,
and she was up there in the mountains
of an unblinking gaze with her one
unending sentence, all the lights
in the building blazing, heat pouring
from the windows and steaming
over the rooftops of your town,
my town, like rows of books
facing down. The need for sleep
twisted through us like weather extremes
and broke off the hands of the clocks.
Who knows how long I spent
gazing into her fiery eye,
the pin point of the turning world.

When she started to crawl
parts of our own lives crawled to a stop
and parts of us got up and walked for the first time.
She was everywhere like god, like real people,
and we were placing gates and stairs
working out sentences, placing punctuation.

Julia Darling

A Short Manifesto For My City

This city shall treasure its pedestrians
and its small places, its irregular shops.

It shall hang onto its pink lanes, its towers,
Dog Leap stairs and Pudding Chares.

And the city shall never try to be Barcelona,
or dress itself in luxury underwear.

Let it be salty, and rusty with iron,
keep secrets beneath its potent river

and be proud to be radical, afraid
of refurbishment. It doesn't need fireworks,

or Starbucks; for it knows its interior.
Let it always be ready to take off its hat.

My city is hard stone, canny and clever.
Don't give it a mirror. Let it be itself.

Mark Doty

HEAVEN FOR PAUL

The flight attendant said,
We have a mechanical problem with the plane,
and we have contacted the FAA for advice,

and then, *We will be making an emergency landing in Detroit,*

and then, *We will be landing at an air force base in Dayton,*
because there is a long runway there, and because
there will be a lot of help on the ground.

Her voice broke slightly on the word *help,*
and she switched off the microphone, hung it back on its hook,
turned to face those of us seated near her,
and began to weep.

Could the message have been more clear?
Around us people began to cry themselves,
or to pray quietly, or to speak to those with whom
they were travelling, saying the things that people
would choose to say to one another before
an impending accident of uncertain proportions.

It was impossible to hear, really, the details
of their conversations – it would have been wrong to try –
but one understood the import of the tones of voice
everywhere around us, and we turned to each other,

as if there should have been some profound things to be
    imparted,
but what was to be said seemed so obvious and clear:
that we'd had a fine few years, that we were terrified
for the fate of our own bodies and each other's,
and didn't want to suffer, and could not imagine

the half-hour ahead of us. We were crying a little
and holding each other's hands, on the armrest;
I was vaguely aware of a woman behind us, on the aisle,
who was startled at the sight of two men holding hands,

and I wondered how it could matter to her, now,
on the verge of this life – and then I wondered how it
   could matter to me
that she was startled, when I flared on that same margin.

The flight attendant instructed us in how to brace
for a crash landing – to remove our glasses and shoes
and put our heads down, as we did long ago, in school,
in the old days of civil defence. We sat together, quietly.
And this is what amazed me: Paul,

who of the two of us is the more nervous,
the less steadily grounded in his own body,
became completely calm. Later he told me

how he visualised his own spirit
stepping from the flames, and visited,
in his picturing, each person he loved,
and made his contact and peace with each one,

and then imagined himself turning toward
what came next, an unseeable *ahead*.
                              For me,
it wasn't like that at all. I had no internal composure,

and any ideas I'd ever entertained about dying
seemed merely that, speculations flown now
while my mind spiralled in a hopeless sorrowful motion,

sure I'd merely be that undulant fuel haze
in the air over the runway, hot chemical exhaust,
atomised, no idea what had happened to me,

what to do next, and how much of the next life
would I spend (as I have how much of this one?)
hanging around an airport. I thought of my dog,

and who'd care for him. No heaven for me
only the unimaginable shape of not-myself –
and in the chaos of that expectation,

without compassion, unwilling,
I couldn't think beyond my own dissolution.
What was the world without me to see it?

And while Paul grew increasingly radiant,

the flight attendant told us it was time to crouch
into the positions we had rehearsed,
the plane began to descend, wobbling,

and the tires screeched against the runway;
burning down all but a few feet of five miles of asphalt
before it rolled its way to a halt.

We looked around us, we let go
the long held breath, the sighs and exhalations,
Paul exhausted from the effort of transcendence,

myself too pleased to be breathing to be vexed
with my own failure, and we were still sitting and beginning to
    laugh
when the doors of the plane burst open,

and large uniformed firemen came rushing down the aisles,
shouting *Everybody off the plane, now, bring nothing with you,*
leave the plane immediately

– because, as we'd learn in the basement
of the hangar where they'd brought us,
a line of tornadoes was scouring western Ohio,
approaching the runway we'd fled.

At this point it seemed plain: if God intervenes
in history, it's either to torment us
or to make us laugh, or both, which is how

we faced the imminence of our deaths the second time.
I didn't think once about my soul, as we waited in line,
filing into the hangar, down into the shelter

– where, after a long while, the National Guard would bring us
boxes and boxes of pizza, and much later, transport us, in buses,
to complimentary hotel rooms in Cincinnati.

Carol Ann Duffy

ABSENCE

Then the birds stitching the dawn with their song
have patterned your name.

Then the green bowl of the garden filling with light
is your gaze.

Then the lawn lengthening and warming itself
is your skin.

Then a cloud disclosing itself overhead
is your opening hand.

Then the first seven bells from the church
pine on the air.

Then the sun's soft bite on my face
is your mouth.

Then a bee in a rose is your fingertip
touching me here.

Then the trees bending and meshing their leaves
are what we would do.

Then my steps to the river are text to a prayer
printing the ground.

Then the river searching its bank for your shape
is desire.

Then a fish nuzzling the water's throat
has a lover's ease.

Then a shawl of sunlight dropped in the grass
is a garment discarded.

Then a sudden scatter of summer rain
is your tongue.

Then a butterfly paused on a trembling leaf
is your breath.

Then the gauzy mist relaxed on the ground
is your pose.

Then the fruit from the cherry tree falling on grass
is your kiss, your kiss.

Then the day's hours are theatres of air
where I watch you entranced.

Then the sun's light going down from the sky
is the length of your back.

Then the evening bells over the rooftops
are lovers' vows.

Then the river staring up, lovesick for the moon,
is my long night.

Then the stars between us are love
urging its light.

Paul Durcan

THE FAR SIDE OF THE ISLAND

Driving over the mountain to the far side of the island
I am brooding neither on what lies ahead of me
Nor on what lies behind me. Up here
On top of the mountain, in the palm of its plateau,
I am being contained by its wrist and its fingertips.

The middle of the journey is what is at stake –
Those twenty-five miles or so of in-betweenness
In which marrow of mortality hardens
In the bones of the nomad. From finite end
To finite end, the orthopaedics of mortality.

Up here on the plateau above the clouds,
Peering down on the clouds in the valleys,
There are no fences, only moorlands
With wildflowers as far as the eye can see;
The earth's unconscious in its own pathology.

Yet when I arrive at the far side of the island
And peer down at the outport on the rocks below,
The Atlantic Ocean rearing raw white knuckles,
Although I am globally sad I am locally glad
To be about to drive down that corkscrew road.

Climbing down the tree-line, past the first cottage,
Past the second cottage, behind every door
A neighbour. It is the company of his kind
Man was born for. Could I have known,
Had I not chanced the far side of the island?

Jennie Feldman

BONFIRE ON THE BEACH

Tragedy was short-lived:
where the pine log had split its sides

dying, a spider elbowed out
and flared a brief nothing.

Old as planets the four faces
round this sun. A smudge

on the sand, like a mistake,
will mean we've gone.

Alan Gillis

Don't You

1

I was working as a waitress in a cocktail bar,
that much is true. But even then I knew I'd find
myself behind the wheel of a large automobile,
or in a beautiful house, asking myself, well,
if sweet dreams are made of these, why don't I travel
the world and the seven seas to Rio, and dance there
in the sand, just like a river twisting through the dusty land?
For though you thought you were my number one,
this girl did not want to have a gun for hire,
no bright spark who was just dancing in the dark.

2

You were working as a waitress in a cocktail bar,
when I met you. And I believed in miracles:
every step you took, I was watching you.
I asked for your name, tipped you again and again
and you said, Don't – don't you want me
to fetch you a drink that would turn your pink mouth blue?
Don't you think this tenth tiny chaser is ten times bigger
  than you?
Don't you talk about places and people you will never know.
Don't you symbolize femininity by use of the letter O.
And I said, Don't you want me, baby? Don't you want me...

Jane Griffiths

CLAIRVOYANCE

Spring, and the river is rising: claxon
of geese, shrill of forsythia's five
stems forked in a glass jar,
and wavering. An oak sprouts waterfalls,

the house paw-talks in the roof at night,
there are toothmarks in the butter.
Industrious, bees batten on the carpet,
the upholstery, signing like mutes,

and rain nets me in. Your messages slip
through with arrowed wakes, migratory
in formation. You say there's snow,
you've banked an enormous fire,

have been out walking among the trees
I couldn't name, gauging their sextant angles
with the measured glance of a fisherman.
That you'll drive by another river, fetch

bread, jalapenos, liquor. Unpacking,
the brown paper bag spells contraband;
in your glass room the whisky glows
amber through a forest in silhouette

like fish bright among water-weed,
the current under ice. It will be late there.
Here tower bells tumble as turbines.
You'll be heaping up coals before sleeping.

I open all the windows. Early light
rimes the bees' carpet of fur.

Paul Groves

MAN AND BOY

My father used to get a six-inch nail,
position it above the little 'eye',
and give one hammer stroke. If all went well
he would not need another to gain entry
to the hidden heart. Maraca-like,

it had been shaken roughly near an ear.
Once I had heard that distant inner lake
it became time to taste its magic water.
The coconut smacked of an old ape's breast,
fibrous and alien. Spike extracted,

my father raised the fruit as if a blest
offering, and carefully enacted
the ancient ritual. I sampled next.
We changed to sucklings at a sacred pap.
No word was said. This went below all text

into a tribal memory. The sap
was drained, and then the butchery began.
The wooden ball was placed on a flat stone
and axed into two halves. He lifted one
and left the second portion, which was mine.

Jen Hadfield

Song of Parts

This is how the catch is gutted –
you diddle the knife down fatty silver,
fingernail-deep, the broad blade's tip.
Slow burgundies stain the enamel sink.
Mackerel hoop and harden in your grip.
With tugsome bravery you yank
the gut-end, coda of a bloodless old song;
the silty fruits coddled away;
the clean fish and its swimbladder,
like a tigerlily,
                    on the cutting board

John Hartley Williams

BIRDCLOUD
(*'Vogelwolke'*, Ernst Meister)

An evening
starred with starlings…
Were that wordplay
it also brings out
truth,
so blackly twittering,
an unheard-of-ness
in the labyrinth.

It must
be Autumn: a furrowing
of the brow,
the birdcloud
rising
from fouled treetops

to take
northwards, an
incomprehensible direction.

David Herd

SEPTEMBER IITH, 2001

Worked in the morning.

Watched TV.

Geoffrey Hill

from SCENES FROM COMUS, *part 2*

18

This is a fabled England, vivid
in winter bareness; bleakly comforting,
the faded orchard's hover of grey-green.
We have come home, say, all is well between us.
Sharp-shining berries bleb a thorn, as blood
beads on a finger or a dove's breast pierced
by an invisible arrow to the heart.

Jackie Kay

LATE LOVE

How they strut about, people in love,
how tall they grow, pleased with themselves,
their hair, glossy, their skin shining.
They don't remember who they have been.

How filmic they are just for this time.
How important they've become – secret, above
the order of things, the dreary mundane.
Every church bell ringing, a fresh sign.

How dull the lot that are not in love.
Their clothes shabby, their skin lustreless;
how clueless they are, hair a mess; how they trudge
up and down streets in the rain,

remembering one kiss in a dark alley,
a touch in a changing-room, if lucky, a lovely wait
for the phone to ring, maybe, baby.
The past with its rush of velvet, its secret hush

already miles away, dimming now, in the late day.

Tim Kendall

DIVORCE

He intends to write of his parents' divorce.

He remembers the view to the sea, and the rock vanishing at high tide. He is four years old. He owns a container of coins with pictures of ships, Spanish galleons. He strokes them and afterwards his hands smell of rust. Coins cold on his tongue. He feels the feel of swallowing one, the feel all the way down.

He intends to write of his parents' divorce. A hand through glass to reach a lock. Glass in the hallway, and blood.

He locks himself in the bathroom, but only by accident, and his parents are calling. The door almost bursts. He washes his hands, they smell of rust.

He remembers the rock. It looms, it shrinks, a white fist, then there's nothing, really.

R F Langley

This morning in November in the bar
of the Angel there is an open fire.
I tell you this so you imagine it
as though the bar in the Angel were a
place that has been given to itself, full
of itself, filled with the things there are in
here, such as the fire. Not the words but the
flames. This is quite possible though you know
that what you have of it, its hum and pop,
could not be prior to the poem. You
don't take shelter in the darkness and the
cold of open countryside which, in the
morning, will turn out to be inside the
giant's glove. You sit down at a table
by the window where you can feel the flames,
take off your gloves, wait for Louise, who comes
through the doors into such places, those given
to themselves. You still enjoy the way she
does, and here she is. Grey eyes. Black hair. Go
for the gloves. Fashioned by trolls, the food is
tied up in impenetrable iron.
The cat is stuck into the shape of sleep
and can't be levered off the floor. Your tongue
proves chocolate dust on cappuccino
froth. It's all as heavy and as hard as
that. But it holds good. There is some truth in
every bit of it. Louise can help, things
on her mind, her fingers lost around the
coffee cup. The good spectators will now
imagine someone facing her across
the table, where otherwise there would be
empty space. Someone is called to work on
a complete Louise, lever her off the

floor, fix her in iron, put her amongst
grey eyes, black hair, and seat her opposite.
That will be me, facing Louise, feeling
the fire inside the Angel bar, inside
the giant's glove, the window to my left.
I will arrive precisely when Louise
picks up her cup, touches the iron, wakes
the terrific cat, and both of us are
given to ourselves, together with trolls,
perhaps, and incredible November.

Michael Longley

THE HOLLY BUSH
in memory of Dorothy Molloy

Frosty Carrigskeewaun. I am breaking ice
Along the salt marsh's soggy margins
And scaring fieldfares out of the holly bush
And redwings, their consorts, chestnut-brown
Flashing one way, chestnut-red another,
Fragments of the January dawn-light
That Killary focuses on the islands
Before it clears the shoulder of Mweelrea.
Caher Island and Inishturk are frosty too.
In the shortlived spotlight they look like cut-
Outs and radiate apricot from within.
I learn of your death in this weather and
Of your book arriving the day after,
Your first and last slim volume. Dorothy,
You read your poems just once and I was there.
The poets you loved are your consorts now.
A hundred or more golden plovers turn
And give back dawn-light from their undersides.
The edge of the dunes wears a shiny fringe.

Patrick McGuinness

A History of Doing Nothing

And who would write it?
                                        Its first historians
were bemused: it moved, yes, but imperceptibly;
used Time as action did, took place along
the hours, the days, needing somewhere to unfold
like all the things it wasn't. The instruments
designed to trap it could not keep up;
the mind slid off it like water on an oily cloth.
In photographs it was the shadow that seemed
to leak from motion, so that each moving
thing looked always in the company
of its ghost, its own grey opposite.

In wars, it was inferred from the slack rigging
of the warships, the flotillas nuzzling at their moorings;
Heraclitus knew: into the same nothing
nobody stepped twice. Physics was born
when they found that all things bring
a corresponding nothing into being;
metaphysics when they learned that in
a perfect world each thing done
aspired to the same thing left undone.

Its founding epic still used heroes, battles, temples…
only for the space that lay between them. Events?
no; the gaps that separate events,
the hungerless white dreams between awakenings,
slow afternoons that ran aground on boredom.
Its sacred books, pristine from inattention,
promised a paradise where all the squandered energy,
dissipated talents, missed appointments
with destiny or with friends would fuse
in one infinity of cancellation;

where not to have been born was only second best.

What of the doers of nothing?
                          To the naked eye
they seemed no different from ourselves, surveyed
the low comedy that was activity from beds
or armchairs, suspended in their dusky lives
as the world turns in the emptiness that holds it steady.
Like us, they folded back into Time's pleats
before going, traceless, where the dead go,
soft-footed in the unresisting dark.

Michael Mackmin

DOLMEN

A thick blue string was tied
across the track, and in the wood
the place itself was fenced with wire,
barbed, more than human height
which in itself had echoes, memories.
A narrow gate of upright angle iron
led us in. The dome stone, grey,
curved like a skull's top,
was poised on four thick teeth:
there was a space beneath.
She clambered under while I stood,
watched the aspen leaves.
The sound is different here she said.
I went under too and heard.

Where once we would have kissed,
stripped, and she'd have slid onto me,
shuddered, and so on, we sat in stillness
till, spooked by thinking
(the weight of time – had I locked the car?),
we crawled out of the shadow,
found the wood thick with the black buzz
of flies, walked to where an oriole scolded
high in an oak. What was it then?

A shelter for the dead for when –
as it may – the sky's skull cracks and falls?
Or one of many things made to catch earth's
breath, and change the shape of sound?

Mazen Makkouk

ON BUYING A PAIR OF POINTED SHOES
for Saher

Even you were surprised I bought them,
you who live in the oldest part of the old city,
near the Mosque of the Crows, no less,
in whose wall is embedded a Hittite stone,
and walking to your house one has to pass
the stalls overflowing with innards, and take care
not to slip on the stones:
those are puddles I wouldn't fall into
no matter what their cultural value.

The shopkeeper and his boy also were surprised
the boy wearing a look of happy complicity
as he rushed off to find my size.
The shopkeeper sensed I needed no persuasion,
but, playing his part, assured me that
the bird design on this one was now the fashion.

In a politer part of town
a taxi asks in passing,
to the village?
Girls on the university bus
look at the shoes and then at each other.
But notoriety is not what I am after
(although it has its pleasures. Remember the British Council?)

'A lonely impulse of delight'
is how I might have described what drove me to buy them
to the pretty secretary there.

They are not meant to invite, but hang simply in rows
in the dusty and dimly-lit shops of Bab-en-Nasr.
Glasses of tea go into their making,

and much hunched conversation,
and on the foot they are snug, and squeaky.

And when in the shoe corner of some mosque
I deposit them with the other shoes,
who is to know that they don't belong
to some old Aleppo gentleman?

When I leave with the crowd, I play the part,
stowing the shoes under my arm with a deft
movement, hoping that in the hustle my act will pass,
or that at least, if it comes, the stare
will be kind. For if here they don't forgive, then where?

Glyn Maxwell

RAUL AT HAPPY HOUR

I swear you guys are keeping us in business.
What is it with you Brits, you ruled the world
one time, how did you do that *drunk*? I tell you,
you know it's our turn now, but we don't do that.
We walk the thin white line, you ought to try it.
You lovely ladies gonna need ID.

I said you ladies gonna need ID.
You're Britney freakin Spears, I'm out of business
if I serve you. Here, Joey, you should try it,
waking up some morning in the world
all kind of clean inside? Only don't do that
while I'm still working here. Hey, I tell you,

and don't you say a word if I do tell you
you Brits – hey Love-of-my-life, this your ID?
Like twelve she looks. Fourteen tops. Check that.
She's legal, or some guy in the forgery business
We Salute You. *Rum? What a wicked world.*
Sweetheart, you're gonna suffer. Okay try it.

Clint I might be leaving. *Go on try it.*
Moving on up, I feel I ought to tell you.
Wasn't so shabby. Gotta go up in the world
of catering or – *guys, need to see ID* –
you're fucked excuse my language. That's the business.
It's in the nature. So, I'm waiting on that,

this offer. In the mean time this and that.
If ever I see a way you know I try it,
always I do. If it's pleasure, or it's business,
always jump, don't stand there. Was that you,
Joey, way back when? Can I see ID,
Mr Stone, I'm kidding! No that's my world.

Keep moving you can *move* the goddam world!
Stand still, you wanna stand still, you *do* that –
you lovely ladies gonna need ID –
nothing comes of nothing. Gotta try it,
right? – *hey I'm from Cleveland like you,*
Cheyenne, you married? What? It's all *my business!* –

I have to try it on, you know, in my world.
'Mind your own damn business.' You hear that?
Your ID, kid, is *way* hotter than you.

Geraldine Mills

PEARL

The grit that found
its way in under your nail
turned the finger septic,

you a young girl sent over
on the boat with your brothers
to toil the dark harvest,

pickers bent over like question marks,
knuckles skinned,
trawling the ridges for tubers

only fit for sleep
after bowls of what
you'd picked, boiled,

sleeping on straw in the women's bothy
to dream of gloves
with jewel buttons, necklaces.

What happened after that
is gone with you
except that the nail abscessed,

the bed of it infected;
no oyster way to mantle it layer over layer
of nacre, reverse its taint to lustre, pearl,

instead lanced and lanced again
it lost its memory
to grow straight

but ridged and beaked like abalone
grew a further eighty years
among the perfect others of your right hand

and funny how laying you out,
the undertaker painted it
mother-of-pearl, lustrous, absorbing light.

Esther Morgan

ARE YOU HOMESICK FOR THE HOUSE OF CARDS?
  Charles Simic, *School for Visionaries*

How can you be
when you've never escaped the palace of family
where assassins hide behind tapestries
and wolfhounds are digging in the cellar?
You feel at home and sick

in your hand-me-down skin,
watching the king flushed with vintage anger
while Jack, hunch-backed by shadows,
crouches in the corner juggling bone-handled knives.
The dark glitter of this game

keeps the queen sleeved in grief,
her tears twinned in the bedroom mirror
as she locks up something
in an iron-bound chest
and throws away the key.

You dream of teeth grinding
in a rusted lock, of leaving one night
by the secret staircase, with nothing
but a small warmth held tight beneath your cloak,
red and beating.

Sinéad Morrissey

GENETICS

My father's in my fingers, but my mother's in my palms.
I lift them up and look at them with pleasure –
I know my parents made me by my hands.

They may have been repelled to separate lands,
to separate hemispheres, may sleep with other lovers,
but in me they touch where fingers link to palms.

With nothing left of their togetherness but friends
who quarry for their image by a river,
at least I know their marriage by my hands.

I shape a chapel where a steeple stands.
And when I turn it over,
my father's by my fingers, my mother's by my palms

demure before a priest reciting psalms.
My body is their marriage register.
I re-enact their wedding with my hands.

So take me with you, take up the skin's demands
for mirroring in bodies of the future.
I'll bequeath my fingers, if you bequeath your palms.
We know our parents make us by our hands.

Paul Muldoon

As I had held Carlotta close
that night we watched some Xenophon
embedded with the 5th Marines
in the old Sunni triangle
make a half-assed attempt to untangle
the ghastly from the price of gasoline.
There was a distant fanfaron
in the Nashville sky where the wind
had now drawn itself up and pinned
on her breast a Texaco star.
'Why,' Carlotta wondered, 'the House of *Tar*?
Might it have to do with the gross
imports of crude oil Bush will come clean on
only when the Tigris comes clean?'

Lucy Newlyn

BAKING

Strange, her knack for turning up
these thirty-odd years
when I least expect her:

ironing, folding the sheets,
or most often baking cakes;
so that I stop to consider

how, involuntarily,
sounds, thoughts, smells, shapes
are habits arranged round her face.

Suddenly, through a half-open
window, comes warm layered scent
of syringa, bonfires, mown grass.

How readily the present folds away:
everything standing back
from itself, unchanged –

the terrace from the road,
the house a long way off down the garden,
rooms deepening through the hall,

light falling in its usual place
by the kitchen window
where she stands, baking cakes.

Someone down the terrace
is mowing their lawn, and our side
of the street is in cool quiet shadow.

Front to back, home lengthens,
making what is familiar
past, particular, necessary, strange.

Conor O'Callaghan

COVENTRY

On a night as clear and warm as tonight,
in 1941, a stray German squadron
with a war to win and a radar on the blink
mistook the quays of neutral Seatown
for the lights of greater Coventry.

On a night as clear and warm as tonight –
when she has gone into an almighty huff
and taken the chat over heaven-knows-what
(or something of nothing with a bit of fluff)
and my lot once again is the box-room futon,
the guest duvet –
                    I am inclined to think
perhaps the Luftwaffe after all were spot on,
and would give my eye-teeth for butterfly bombs
to fall into this silence I have been sent to.

Peter Porter

Mi Diverto

And if the world be mad
And tied up to success
With hope of trading good for bad
Dispersed as 'more means less' –

And generations strive
To push their children on
So one blood line of all might thrive
In one dominion,

And this be plain to each
Since History sat down
To plan anew on hill or beach
A truer sort of town,

Then why contrive an art
Touching not the least
A juster, fairer, kinder start
Or sure place at the feast,

And fashion at the desk
Instead thought's sounds and shapes
To make what consequence at best
Will buy in books and tapes

Unless it is to please
The oldest animal,
A self of brain and jointed knees,
The bored obsessional.

Sheenagh Pugh

THE BEREAVEMENT OF THE LION-KEEPER
for Sheraq Omar

Who stayed, long after his pay stopped,
in the zoo with no visitors,
just keepers and captives, moth-eaten,
growing old together.

Who begged for meat in the market-place
as times grew hungrier,
and cut it up small to feed him,
since his teeth were gone.

Who could stroke his head, who knew
how it felt to plunge fingers
into rough glowing fur, who has heard
the deepest purr in the world.

Who curled close to him, wrapped in his warmth,
his pungent scent, as the bombs fell,
who has seen him asleep so often,
but never like this.

Who knew that elderly lions
were not immortal, that it was bound
to happen, that he died peacefully,
in the course of nature,

but who knows no way to let go
of love, to walk out of sunlight,
to be an old man in a city
without a lion.

Sally Read

INSTRUCTION

Check: water, soap, a folded sheet, a shroud.
Close cubicle curtains; light's swallowed
in hospital green. Our man lies dense
with gravity: an arm, his head, at angles
as if dropped from a great height. There is
a fogged mermaid from shoulder to wrist,
nicotine-stained teeth, nails dug with dirt –
a labourer then, one for the women.
A smooth drain to ivory is overtaking
from the feet. Wash him, swiftly, praising
in murmurs like your mother used,
undressing you when asleep. Dry carefully.
If he complained at the damp when alive, dry
again. Remove teeth, all tags, rip off elastoplast –
careful now, each cell is snuffing its lights,
but black blood still spurts. Now,
the shroud (opaque, choirboy ruff), fasten
it on him, comb his hair to the right. Now
he could be anyone. Now wrap in the sheet,
like a parcel, start at his feet. Swaddle (not
tight nor too loose) – it's an art, sheafing
this bundle of untied, heavy sticks. Hesitate
before covering his face, bandaging warm
wet recesses of eyes, mouth. Your hands
will prick – an animal sniffing last traces
of life. Cradle the head, bind it with tape
and when it lolls, lovingly against your chest,
lower it gently as a bowl brimmed with water.
Collect tags, teeth, washbowl. Open
the window, let the soul fly. Through
green curtains the day will tear: cabs, sun-
glare, rain. Remember to check:
tidied bed, emptied cabinet, sheeted form –

observe him recede to the flux between seconds,
the slowness of sand. Don't loiter. Slide
back into the ward's slipstream; pick up
your pace immediately.

Kate Rhodes

REVERSAL

I can see now it was a mistake
to back my car out of the drive.
Since then the road looks historic
and the future's in the mirror, blurred.

I'm tempted to pull over
but the hard shoulder's bumper to bumper,
full of memories, badly parked.
Miles back I saw a man I used to know.

At least this time
I know well enough not to stop.
With each junction towns grow paler,
hotels in candy pink, baby blue.

By the time I reach your house
you'll be straight-backed,
talking clearly, in the lawn print dress
you always wore.

We'll sit in the garden for hours,
watch the shadows shorten.
Tomorrow you'll be alone
on the swings sailing backwards,

or reading stories from right to left.
You won't have to miss me,
by the time morning comes
I won't even be imaginary.

Michael Rosen

from IN THE COLONIE

Hundreds turned up. There were people
here I had never seen. She had been theirs
too, had she? And they had been hers? This
is a life? People come dressed like they never
dress; people who usually walk in straight
lines walking round and about. But hundreds.
So she was part of a lot. There were people
here, strangers, who had believed in her.

Anne Rouse

STARLINGS

wings for wings' sake
　discernible intent is
　　lured lone elipses whose
　　　this ink-dense cursive cast by
　　　as a human cranes to read
　　　　in the dead night to hector
　　　　　the way that thunder will seem
　　　　signs and importunes
　　　　　flexes and rears
　　　　　as the collective animal
　　　　　not for food or a mate
　　　　　　bull on an unseen tether
　　　　　of pilings like a pointilliste
　　　　　choreographed around the axis
　　　　fore this granular hastening un
　　　　clamations without why or where
　　　pupil or arise as thick as a mob's ex
　　to blink and contract like the eye's stung
　　inaudible cyclone monochrome fireworks
　up as flecks of soil start from the loambed
black in their thousands stir and fling themselves
Starlings lift into the air above West Pier

Fiona Sampson

from HOTEL CASINO

A train's long regression:
flatlands sunlight cows
                              the hand

moving away slowly,
                              the relinquished hand
sliding on glass, are a continuing

touch and there are strings between them
strings of atom sensation symbol flying

the length of a concrete platform.

A smear of country beyond closed windows.

The star of broken glass.
Radiance of a taped pane.

        *

The book of remembering of forgetting
fear.
        The wet white screen. Your eye mine

as if touching, dirt
scenting the skin. Sweat seals it

asleep grief-cold in a slick of hair;
language lies around abandoned

and my
      and my
            night-time-wardrobe useless heart
ticker-tickers yours

much that is forbidden touching cheek-bones gently
from the leaning walls.

Carole Satyamurti

THE WOOD TURNER OF JAUBERTIE
for Joel Beyney

At the start of summer, as every year,
I visit the man who makes wooden fruits,
drawn by his house: the timbers chosen
for their slow arrival at that weight;
lime-wash stained ochre, pale terracotta –
pigments the walls needed to be reminded of.
Year by year, from a ruin,
without sell-short solutions,
he is giving the old house back to itself –

the garden too:
not the usual obedient French plot,
but a painter's palette of sweet peas,
poppies, campanula spilling along
curved stone paths; *potager* dense with promise
of pumpkins, haricots, the brilliant orange, yellow
and purple stripes of rare tomatoes.

And I'm drawn to the man himself.
He likes me to see these things,
to share his amazement,
for what's ordinary is joyful to him:
a crimson flowering quince, his whetted tools,
redstarts nesting in the box he made for them.

His craft is unexceptional:
bland apples, neat, symmetrical pears
though, like everything, they're meticulous,
carefully moulded copper stalks,
each calyx carved separately, stoppered in;

then the polishing with linseed oil and beeswax –
the type of object no one really needs, or loves,
but buys out of a vague restlessness.

This year, it's different. Weeping utterly
without embarrassment, he tells me
his nine-year-old died in June –
'aneurysm', he says (he'd never heard of it);
a secret fault that snatched her from him.

How could any words embody
the tread he never stops expecting, the flute lying silent?
How can my words of sympathy be more
than a clatter of small change thrown at catastrophe?
I wish I wasn't there.

He wants to tell me, though:
for months his work seemed pointless,
and dangerous – the tears, the spinning lathe.
But then his hands picked at the briar roots
he'd always scrapped till then and, needing to,
made an apple from the knotted ball.

He shows me – fruits heavier than before:
a blighted gourd, a fig, the lovely grain
wrenched and fissured to reveal
a world of corruption – the whole so compromised
it seems it must collapse, and yet the form holds.

A parallel. Of course – but that thought
doesn't honour the reach by hauled reach, the shift,
compelled by suffering, into terrain where craft
encounters art; finding a vessel for experience,
letting each root lay bare what it knows,
which he now shows me how to understand.

He sets a serious price for them
intending, I think, no one to buy them casually;
but to know that the time it takes
to bring these objects to completion,
and let them go, is a devotedness;
wanting us to see each piece as revelation
salvaged from the lip of what can be borne –
flawed and beautiful, an open question.

David Scott

I would look for signs of weather
at the edges of your clothes, your hands
for the way you hold your pen, and put it down.
I would glance to notice shifts of sun and shadow
of the alternating poetry and prose in you.
I would be curious, acute to sense
such mundane sacraments. The drawing,
small and aerial of Christ, seen
from the Father's desperate height, and the voice
which reached down songs from such tall trees,
would pose questions, as unanswerable
as why the storks so love the towers of Avila.

Peter Sirr

JAMES JOYCE HOMELOANS

At James Joyce's Bistro
James Dunne, proprietor and executive head chef
is to food what
but why not judge for yourself
the inner organs of beasts and fowl
or something a bit more conventional
10% off on presentation of this advert
and not a year goes by that doesn't see
in Adelaide the friends of Willunga and Adlinga
in Rome the ambassador
in Paris meanwhile a potluck picnic
in Fionn McCool's pub, Toronto
in Edwardian clothing
in Philadelphia the Potable Joyce
a watered-down version
in D'Arcy McGee's a singalong
while lemon soap in Sweny's
in Brazil, in Rio Grande do Sul
in the context of the celebration
of 25 years of the student bookshop
and always
in Trieste Zurich Buffalo Syracuse
in Jack Quin's Irish Ale House and Pub
saddle of rabbit with black pudding
lap of mutton
slab of luscious goosebosom
while in Sydney Harbour the *Ulysses* Challenge Yacht Race
and in Melbourne the oxen and the sperm
in the Domed Reading Room
there is no charge for the funeral
but bring a copy if you have one
and proudly supporting the festival
residential mortgages, remortgages

residential investment property or UK property finance
for all your mortgage needs
call us today or stop by!

Paul Stubbs

FROZEN

There are no signs of life here –
this being the after-effect of ice.
It is the countryside chipped out

from chrystal; where the animals
and trees, like objects postponed,
are exhibited as imperceptible forms

in January's only display-case.
There are insects solid in snow
like premonitions of themselves,

and myself nearby on the road,
feeling fragile, and at any second
as if I might suddenly shatter

into a thousand perfect pieces. So then
I dare not move, like each of the other
living species that linger here;

I have been entombed by my own shadow
and my outline is slowly changing,
as if through growing cold

I could eventually find myself,
disfigured, redesigned, and forced
to meander, an eternity, inside

the museum of my own sensations.

George Szirtes

DEAD BABIES
(after Canetti)

There's absolutely nothing between them. The ape
Nurses her dead child as though it were alive,
Tenderly cradles its inert furry shape

And won't let go. It's the first imperative
And must be obeyed. She examines eyes
Mouth, nose and ears, attempts to give

Her baby the breast. She grooms it. Tries
To pick it clean. After a week or so
She leaves off feeding but swats at the flies

That settle on its body and continues to show
Deep interest in its cleanliness. Eventually
She begins to set it down, learns to let go.

It starts to mummify and grows horribly smelly.
Now and then she'll bite at the skin until
A limb drops off, then another. Gradually

It decomposes. Even the skin starts to shrivel.
At last she understands at the back of her head.
She plays with furry objects. There is a subtle

Readjustment. Reverse the roles of the dead.
Turn back the clock. Forgetting is good.
You turn and turn within your tiny bed

Until the back of your mind has understood.

Derek Walcott

from THE PRODIGAL, *part 13*

III

So has it come to this, to have to choose?
The chafe of the breakers' moving marbles,
their lucent and commodious statuary
of turbulent stasis, changing repetition
of drizzling spray that glazes your eyes
like the marble miracles of the Villa Borghese?
Do not diminish in my memory
villages of absolutely no importance,
the rattling bridge over the stone-bright river,
un-ornate churches, chapels in the provinces
of light-exhausted Europe. Hoard, cherish
your negligible existence, your unrecorded history
of unambitious syntax, your clean pools
of unpolluted light over close stones.

Anna Wigley

Dürer's Hare

Still trembling, after five hundred years.
Still with the smell of grass
and the blot of summer rain
on her long, thorn-tipped paws.

Look how thick the fur is,
and how each thistledown hair
catches the light
that glistens even in shadow
from the trimmed plush of the ears.

How did he keep her still?
She was crouched there long enough
for him to trace the fragile hips
and ribs beneath the mink,

to feel the pale edges
of the belly-pouch,
the sprung triggers of the flanks.
The nose shimmers
where the short hairs grow in a rosette.
Go on, touch it.

For she's only here for a moment,
Dürer's hare;
the frame can barely hold her.
Her shadow is a shifting thing,
slippery as a raincloud in wind,
and even as you look,
twitches to be gone.

Gerard Woodward

from ECOPOESIS

7   *Looking Back*

The last millionaires fell from the sky
A century ago. They brought with them
Sad stories of the lives they had left,
How a belief in unicorns and mermaids
Had revived, how the cities had been
Consumed by privet and laurel,
Of sickness, reforestation, wars of religion.

Our children listened entranced
And filled with longing to be
In the world of islands with all
Its rich, rewarding dangers.

Our atmosphere factories have begun
To take on something of the mystery
And charm of pyramids, though
They remind me more of coffee pots,
Or cafetieres, and the pillowy mountains
Behind them with the croissant-shaped
Pebbles that strew their slopes always
Remind me that what we have made here
Is one vast room, world-sized,
Near whose ceiling two acorn
Moons float. Sofa hills. Lamp-stand mountain.
You have to keep a sense of proportion.

Last week the mirrors were ripped
To shreds as they re-entered the atmosphere,
And poured their mirrory rain over a field
The size of the state of Missouri.

Tamar Yoseloff

THE WOMAN WHO DREAMED OF EELS

She is ankle-deep in water,
I'm in the sea, she thinks, then remembers
she's asleep. When they push against her

like cats demanding love,
their faces all snout, heads bobbing,
she knows it's the eel dream again.

She tries to grab them,
just like last night, brings her hand up
empty, smells brine, something gone off.

If I can interpret the dream
while dreaming, they'll go away
and I'll wake up.

So she thinks hard about eels,
dead ones, swimming in liquor,
served at the pie shop.

Just then they fill her mouth,
sour, still alive. She tries to scream
but the eels make her gag.

She wakes, remembers nothing.
There's a strange coating
on her tongue.